PLANET EARTH/INSIDE OUT

GAIL GIBBONS   MORROW JUNIOR BOOKS/NEW YORK

To my aunt Ethel Rueter

ACKNOWLEDGMENTS
The author wishes to thank the following for their careful reading of the text of this book: Nancy Keller, earth science teacher at the Winooski Educational Center, Winooski, Vermont; and, at the geology department of the University of Vermont, Stephen F. Wright, lecturer, and Stephen S. Howe, research geologist.

Watercolors, colored pencils, and India ink were used for the full-color illustrations.
The text type is 17-point Berkeley Old Style.

1 2 3 4 5 6 7 8 9 10

Library of Congress Cataloging-in-Publication Data
Gibbons, Gail.
Planet Earth/inside out/Gail Gibbons.
p. cm.
ISBN 0-688-09680-8 (trade)—ISBN 0-688-09681-6 (library)
1. Earth—Juvenile literature.   [1. Earth.]   I. Title.   QB631.4.G53 1995   550—dc20   94-41926   CIP AC

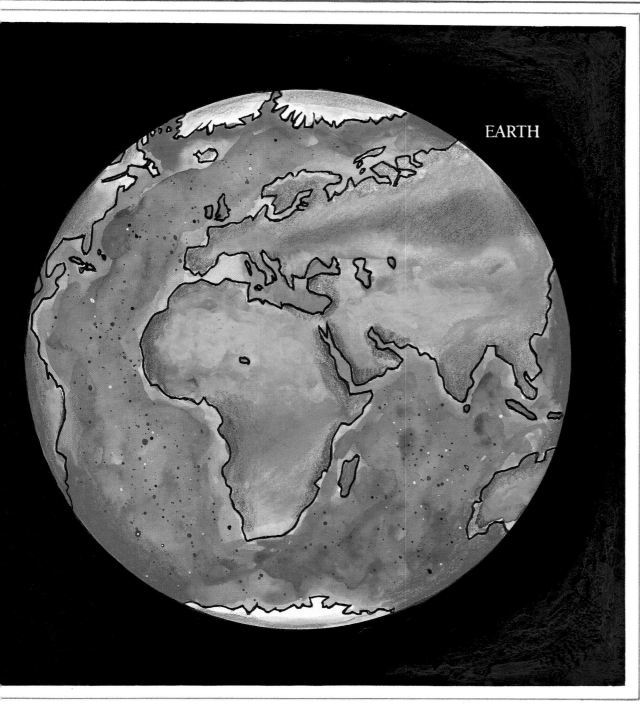

EARTH

Earth is the third planet from the sun. It is the only planet we know of that has just the right environment for plants and animals to live in.

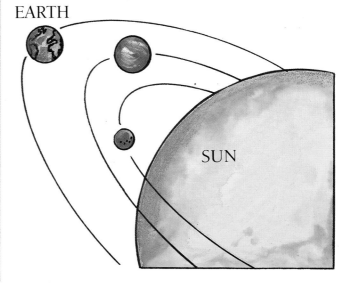

EARTH

SUN

Scientists believe planet Earth was formed about 4.6 billion years ago. They think this happened when a cloud of gases and dust was pulled together by a force called *gravity*. As the cloud spun around, small particles began sticking together. Slowly planet Earth became denser and bigger. The heaviest materials, like iron and nickel, sank to the center.

GRAVITY is an invisible pull that makes objects attract other objects.

At first Earth was very hot. As it cooled down it became hard on the outside. Steam rose from the planet's surface and fell back as rain. Over a long period of time most of Earth became covered with the oceans.

The surface that remained above water became land. Some scientists think that at one time on Earth there was a single massive piece of land, which they call *Pangaea*.

5

PANGAEA

250 MILLION YEARS AGO

50 MILLION YEARS AGO

TODAY

These scientists believe that about 250 million years ago, Pangaea slowly split apart into seven smaller land masses. Between them the oceans created their own shapes. 6

Viewed from space, Earth looks blue. Sunlight shining on the water that covers much of the planet gives Earth its blue color. Also, it looks perfectly round—but it isn't. Instead it is slightly flat at its North and South Poles and bulges a little at its middle, which is called the *equator*. The equator measures 24,912 miles around. It would take 25 million people holding hands to circle it. Earth is very big! Almost three-fourths of Earth's surface is covered by four oceans. The seven land masses are called *continents*.

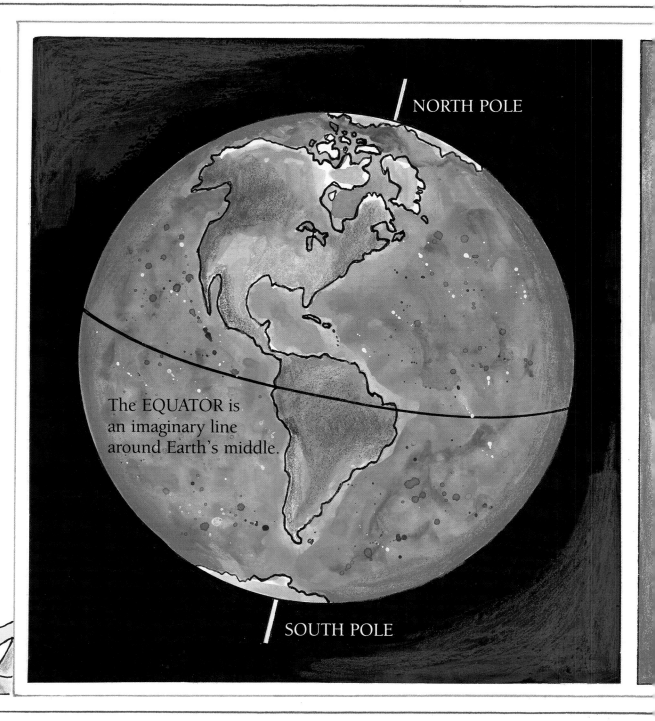

NORTH POLE

The EQUATOR is an imaginary line around Earth's middle.

SOUTH POLE

Planet Earth looks different on the inside. It has four layers. The distance to its center from the planet's surface is about 4,000 miles. At its center is the *inner core*. Scientists believe the inner core is a hot ball of solid iron and nickel, about 1,500 miles across, with temperatures reaching 11,000°F. That's about fifty times as hot as boiling water! It is thought that the inner core is solid because of the huge weight of the rest of Earth pressing all around it.

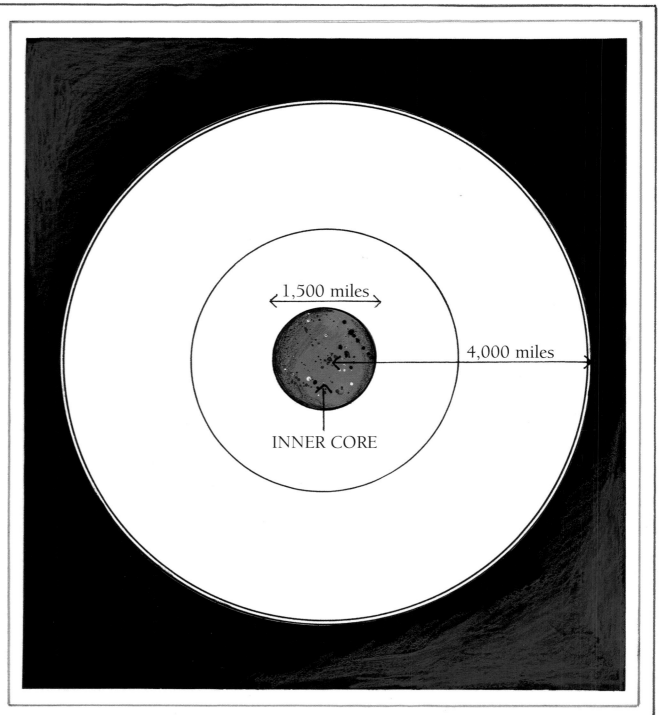

1,500 miles

4,000 miles

INNER CORE

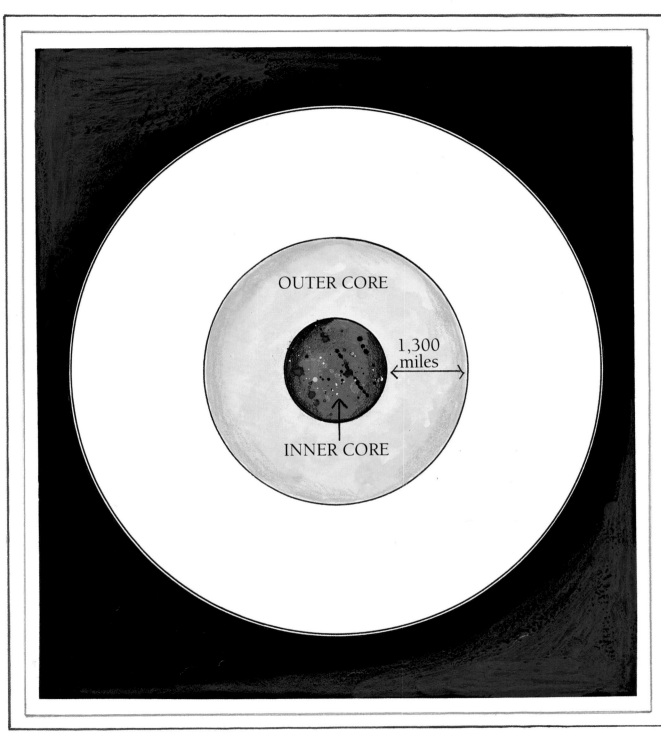

OUTER CORE

INNER CORE

1,300 miles

Outside the inner core is the *outer core*. The outer core is about 1,300 miles thick. That's about how far it is from New York City to Miami, Florida. Scientists believe that the outer core is made up of very hot liquid iron and nickel. At its deepest level it can get to be about 9,000°F. The outer core moves around the inner core very slowly, making electricity that creates the Earth's magnetic field.

Imagine the MAGNETIC FIELD as a huge bar-shaped magnet inside Earth. Its poles lie near the Earth's geographic poles. The magnetic field is what causes a compass needle to point north.

NORTH POLE

SOUTH POLE

Around the outer core is the *mantle.* It is about 1,800 miles thick and can be as hot as 7,500°F. Most of the mantle surrounding the outer core is solid. But some of the outer mantle is made up of partially molten, or melted, rock that moves slowly, like molasses.

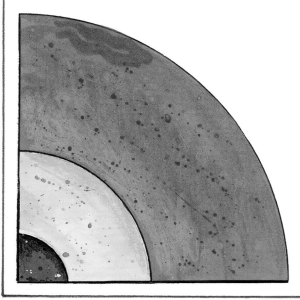

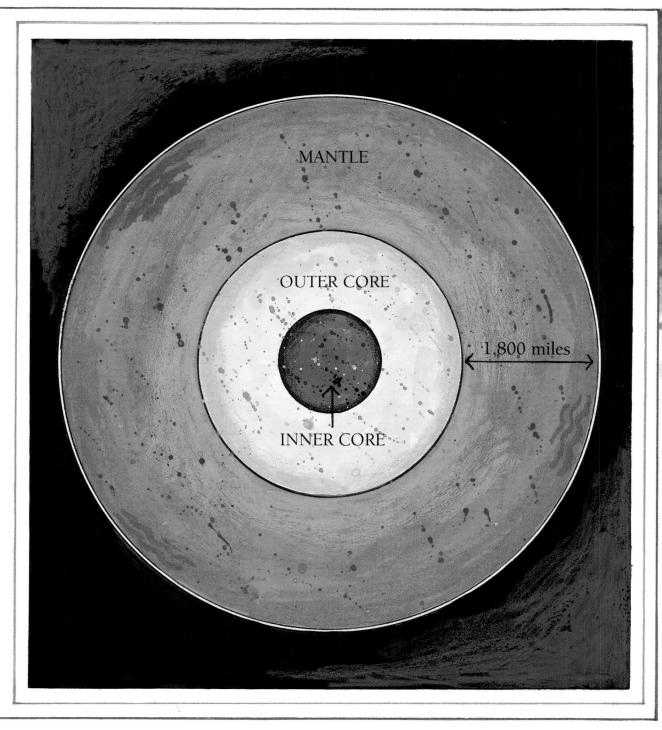

MANTLE

OUTER CORE

1,800 miles

INNER CORE

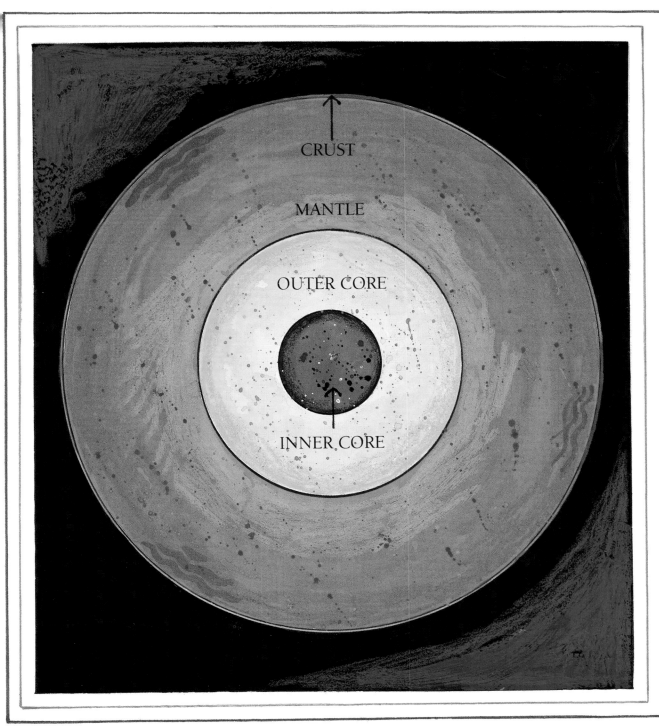

CRUST

MANTLE

OUTER CORE

INNER CORE

Outside the mantle is Earth's *crust*. It is very thin compared to the other layers. Earth's crust is made up of rock and soil. If Earth were the size of a peach, its crust would be about as thin as a peach's skin.

Scientists divide the Earth's crust into two parts, the *oceanic crust* and the *continental crust*. The oceanic crust lies below the oceans. It forms the ocean floor. Some oceanic crust runs underneath the continental crust, which forms the land above sea level.

The crust is not one solid piece. Instead it is split into seven major pieces and many other smaller pieces, called *plates*. Each plate curves to fit the shape of planet Earth. Plates are made up of a thin portion of crust and a thicker portion of outer mantle that lies beneath them. These plates slowly move, because they float on top of partially molten rock. Earth's plates are about forty miles thick under the oceans and about sixty miles thick under the continents.

CONTINENTAL CRUST

SEA LEVEL

OCEANIC CRUST

OUTER MANTLE

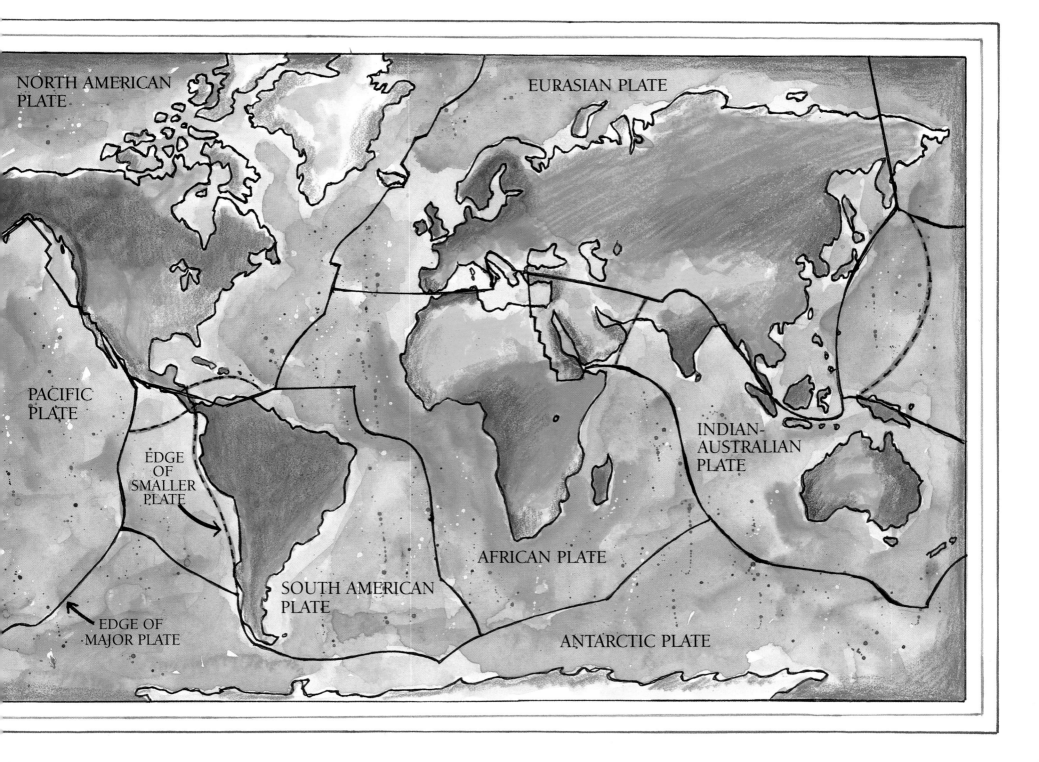

NORTH AMERICAN
PLATE

EURASIAN PLATE

PACIFIC
PLATE

EDGE
OF
SMALLER
PLATE

EDGE OF
MAJOR PLATE

SOUTH AMERICAN
PLATE

AFRICAN PLATE

INDIAN-
AUSTRALIAN
PLATE

ANTARCTIC PLATE

The seven major plates and the other smaller plates of Earth are always moving. When the plates move apart, bump together, overlap, and slide against one another, the surface of Earth moves very slowly. The plates drift at rates of about one to seven inches each year. Planet Earth is in constant motion. That's one reason why we call it the living planet!

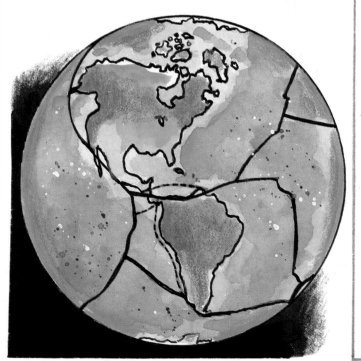

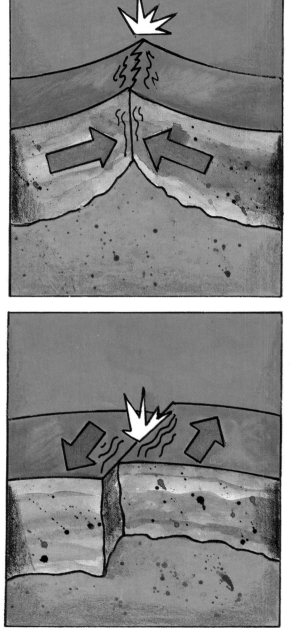

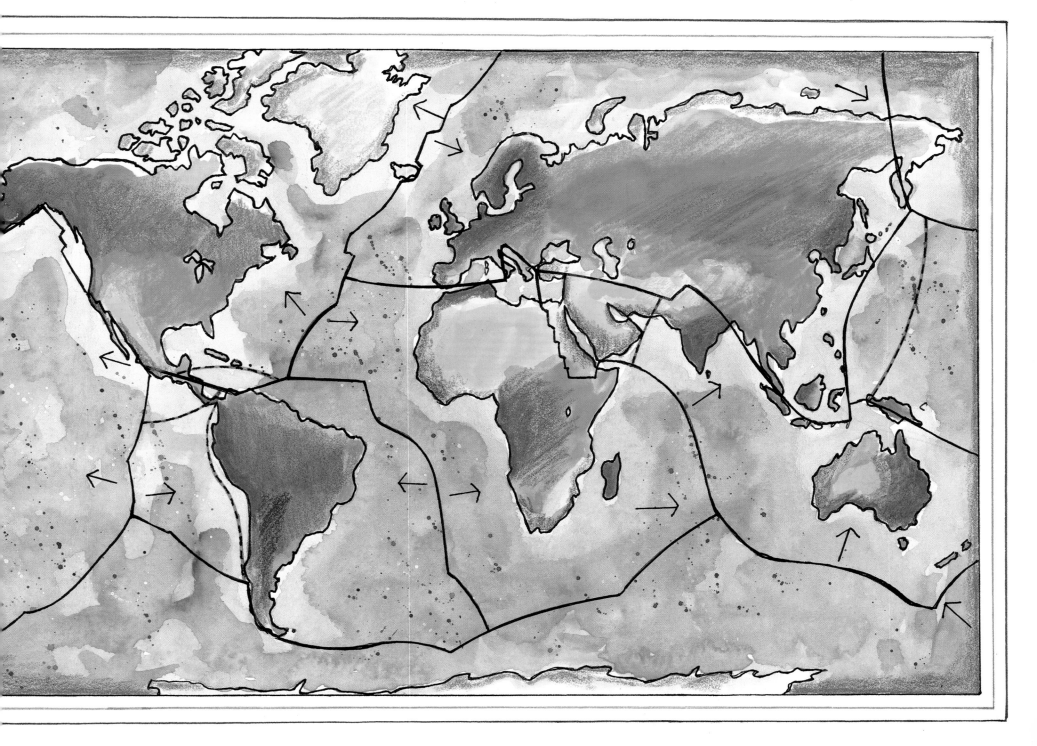

Throughout Earth's crust there are many cracks, called *faults*. Major faults are found near where plates touch. When two plates press against each other, pressure begins to build. When the strain becomes too great, the ground moves suddenly along these faults and an *earthquake* happens. Vibrations move through the Earth. Rocks slip and slide. Sometimes the Earth buckles, or even breaks open.

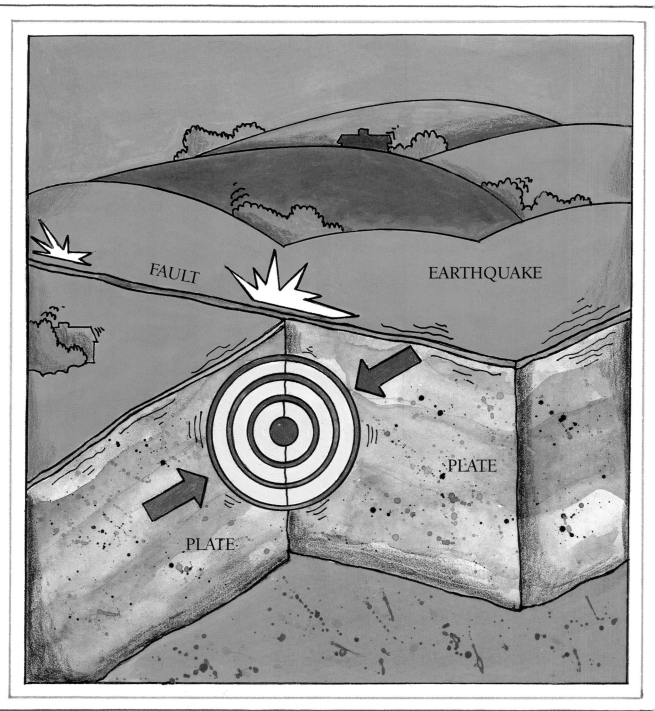

FAULT

EARTHQUAKE

PLATE

PLATE

An earthquake can last from seconds to a few minutes. Sometimes it causes great damage. Scientists can tell how powerful an earthquake is by using instruments that measure the strength of the vibrations, or shock waves, moving through the ground. Often they can predict where earthquakes might happen, but they can't tell when.

15

Volcanoes, like most earthquakes, usually form near where the edges of plates collide. Pressure builds up below the surface, causing cracks or holes to appear in the crust. Then molten rock, called *magma,* and gases push up from deep inside the Earth. This causes an explosion called a *volcanic* 16 *eruption.*

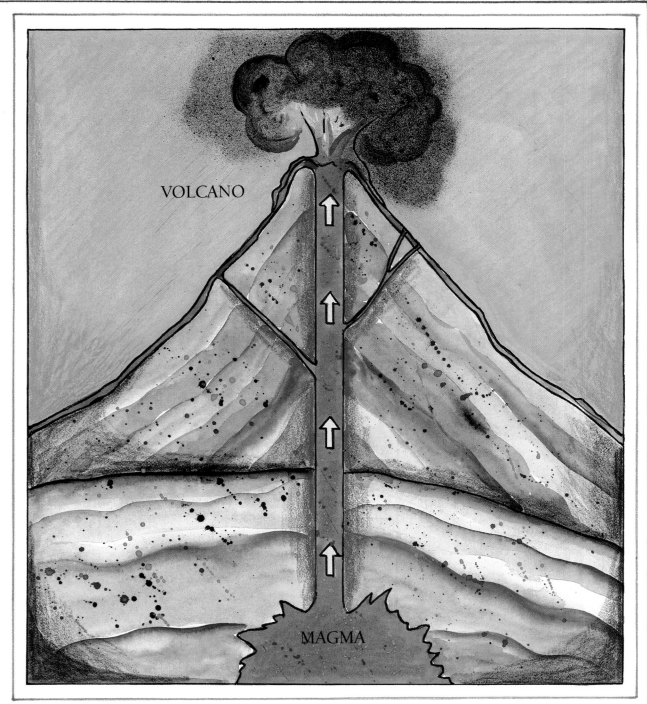

VOLCANO

MAGMA

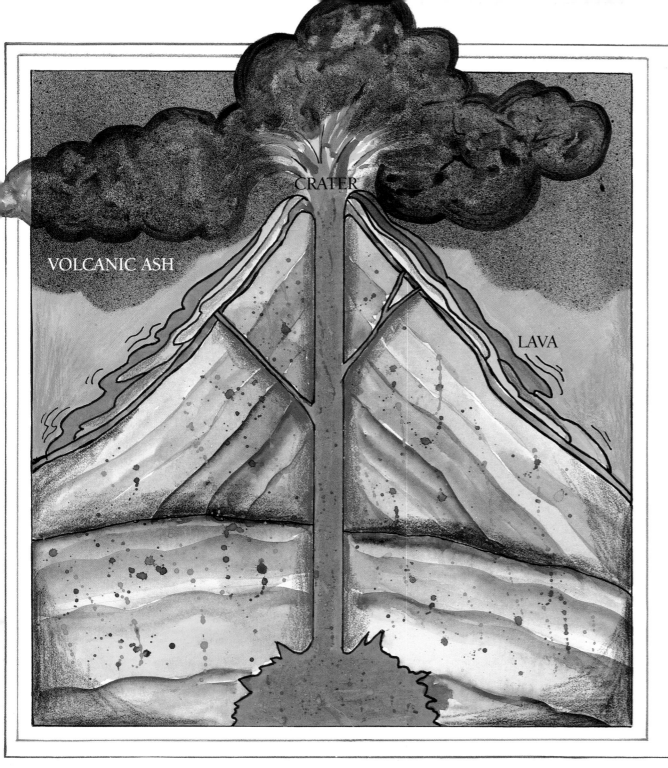

VOLCANIC ASH

CRATER

LAVA

Magma shoots out of the volcano's opening, called the *crater. Volcanic ash* darkens the sky. The magma flows in streams called *lava*. Ash and lava can destroy life for miles around. When the lava cools, it can harden into layers that form steep-sided cone-shaped hills or mountains. Or it can harden into much flatter layers. Active volcanoes erupt often. Dormant volcanoes rest for a long time between eruptions. Extinct volcanoes will never erupt again.

The Earth is ever-changing. Some of the plates beneath the oceans move apart in a process called *seafloor spreading.* As they pull apart, magma from the mantle rises, cools, and becomes solid, adding to the edges of the plates. There are earthquakes and eruptions in the oceans, just like on land. Underwater earthquakes can cause huge waves that are called *tsunamis,* or tidal waves. One was actually recorded to be 278 feet tall!

TSUNAMI

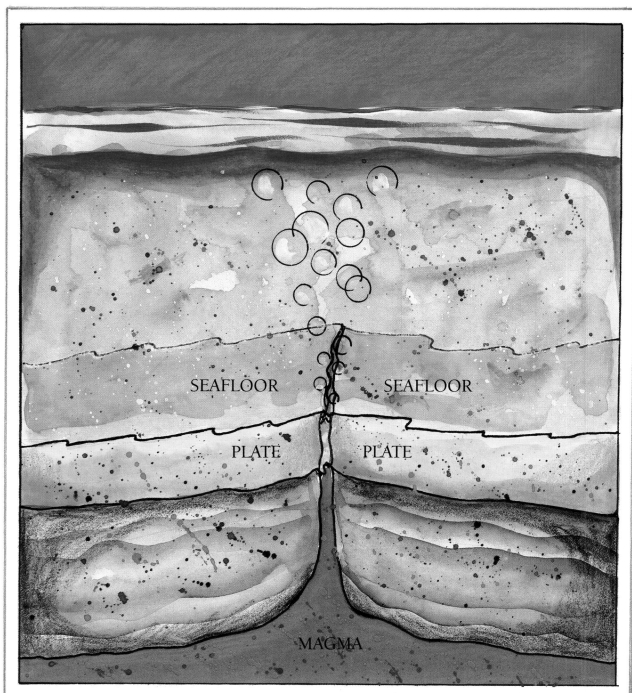

SEAFLOOR   SEAFLOOR

PLATE   PLATE

MAGMA

ISLAND

Oceans can be shallow or very deep, as deep as 36,000 feet! The ocean floor is a landscape that has taken millions of years to form. There are hills, mountains, and flat plains. When the tops of mountains rise above the water they are called *islands*.

The shape of the land, like that of the ocean floor, has formed over millions of years. Great forces have worked to make this happen. When plates crashed into one another, they made the layers of continental crust fold and buckle to form mountain ranges. And when plates pulled apart, they formed depressions in the continental crust called *rift valleys*. Vast ice sheets, called *glaciers*, also changed the Earth's surface. They pushed down over the land, shaping and forming it into valleys, plains, and hills. Most of these changes happen too slowly for people to see.

RIFT VALLEY

GLACIER

Earth's environment is not the same everywhere. This has to do with Earth's climates. Air moves constantly across the planet's surface, driven by the warmth of the sun. The sun warms the Earth more strongly near the equator than at the poles. Depending on the size of the land mass, its location, and the water surrounding it, different climates are created, as well as the weather we experience from day to day.

Plants and animals have lived on Earth for millions of years. When they die, their remains are sometimes embedded in mud. Over many years the mud and remains turn into stone, forming fossils. Fossils are studied to help us understand how life on Earth has changed.

When people began living on Earth, they bettered their lives by learning to use natural resources from the planet's crust. Today we depend on these resources more than ever.

Of all creatures humans have changed planet Earth the most. Many of these changes have been harmful. People have abused Earth's natural resources, and some of Earth's environment has been damaged. Now many people are working to protect Earth and its resources for a better future.

24

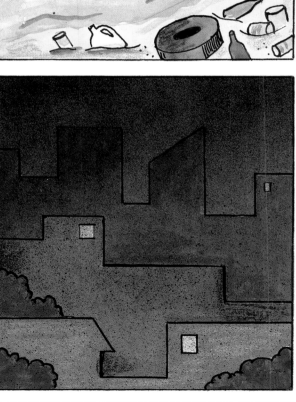

Every place on Earth, from sea to land, should be special to the people who live there. It is our beautiful, living, and ever-changing Earth, inside and out.

ROCKS OF THE EARTH'S CRUST

Igneous rocks are made from molten rock that has cooled one of two ways: slowly, below the surface of the Earth, or quickly, above the surface. That's what gives these rocks their different textures. 26

GRANITE

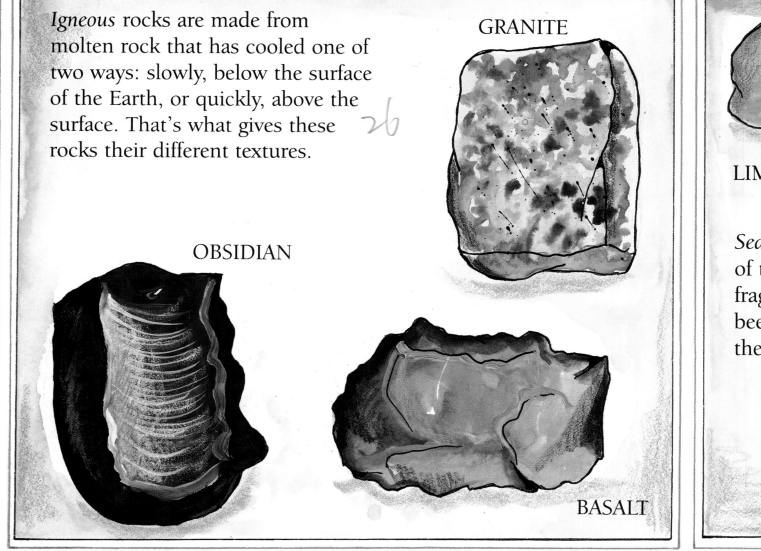

OBSIDIAN

BASALT

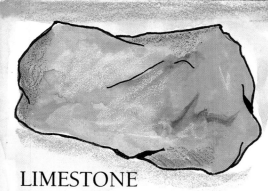

LIMESTONE

Sedimentary rocks most of the time are made from fragments of rock that have been stuck together. Often they contain fossils.

The Earth's crust is made up of different kinds of rocks. All rocks belong to one of three families.

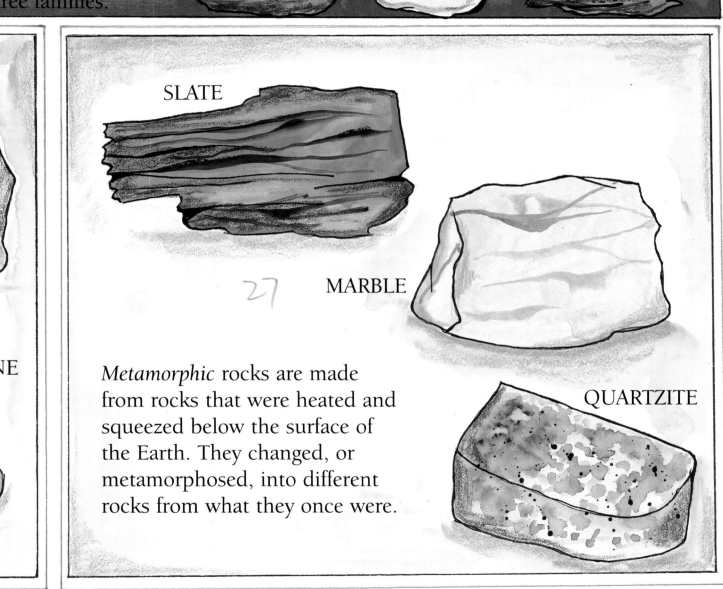

CHALK

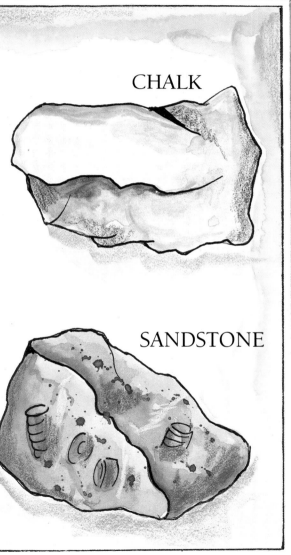

SANDSTONE

SLATE

27

MARBLE

QUARTZITE

Metamorphic rocks are made from rocks that were heated and squeezed below the surface of the Earth. They changed, or metamorphosed, into different rocks from what they once were.

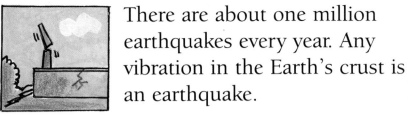

There are about one million earthquakes every year. Any vibration in the Earth's crust is an earthquake.

Someone who studies the Earth is called a *geologist*.

There are more than 600 active volcanoes on Earth.

On the average, twenty to thirty volcanoes erupt each year.

Seashells can be found in rocks high up on some mountains. Over millions of years these rocks were pushed upward as plates collided.

The deserts of the Earth are becoming bigger because of creeping sand dunes. Some of this is caused by climate changes and damage done to the Earth.

Only three percent of all water on Earth is fresh water. The rest is salty.

The rocks of the Earth's crust contain a mixture of over 2,000 minerals.

If all the coastlines of the Earth were straightened out, they would stretch around the equator thirteen times.

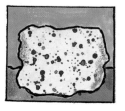

Pumice, a kind of lava rock, is full of many little holes and is light enough to float on water. It is the only rock that can float!